My name is

Jolinda Katherine

Note to Parents and Teachers

This book is a very first introduction to recognizing words. Each page shows one familiar object matched with the word in simple bold type. Colourful artwork encourages the child to name the object and recognize the word.

Oxford University Press, Great Clarendon Street, Oxford OX2 6DP

Oxford is a trade mark of Oxford University Press
Copyright © Oxford University Press 1999
First published 1999
5 7 9 10 8 6 4

A CIP catalogue record for this book is available from the British Library

ISBN 0-19-910718-1 (hardback)
ISBN 0-19-910719-X (paperback)

Printed in Hong Kong

My first book of Words

Illustrated by Julie Park

OXFORD

UNIVERSITY PRESS

apple

baby

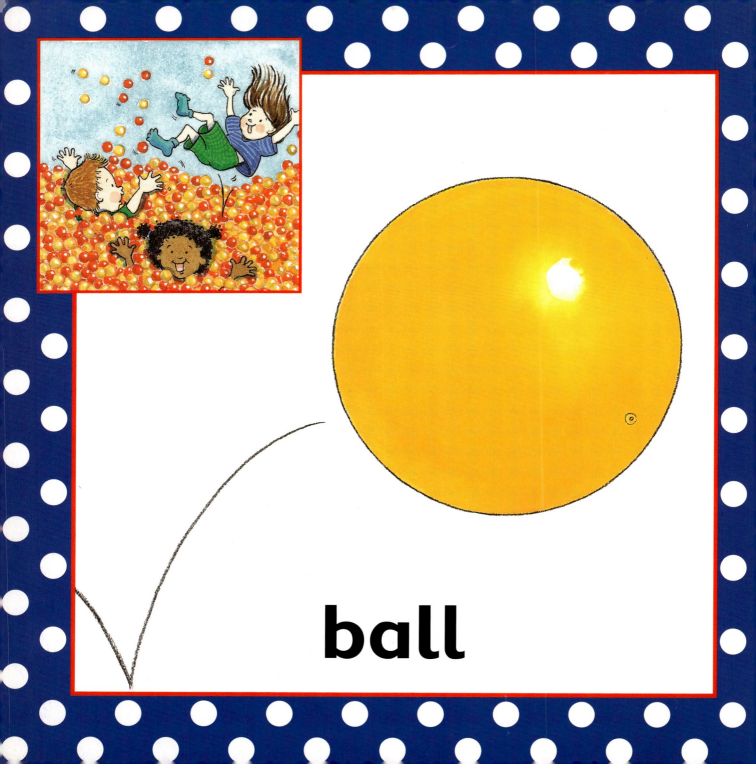

ball

bath

bed

book

cat

dog

duck

elephant

food

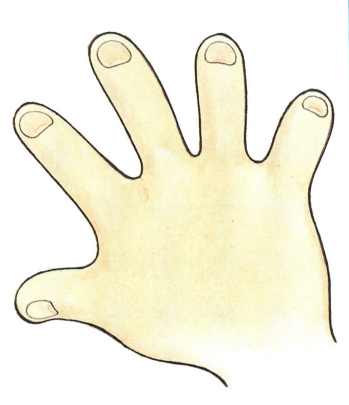

hand

hat

house

jam

keys

milk

mouse

mouth

nose

rabbit

sock

teddy

truck